The Basilica of St. Francis of Assisi

Giorgio Bonsanti

THE BASILICA OF ST. FRANCIS OF ASSISI

GLORY AND DESTRUCTION

Photographs by
Ghigo Roli

Translated from the Italian by
Stephen Sartarelli

HARRY N. ABRAMS, INC., PUBLISHERS

FRIENDS OF ASSISI
WORLD MONUMENTS FUND

The earthquake of September 26, 1997, and its violent aftershocks, caused widespread damage, not only in Assisi, but throughout the surrounding areas of Umbria and the Marches. Many historic buildings in medieval hilltowns were drastically weakened and are now in danger of collapse. Churches, cloisters, and belltowers, as well as important frescoes, altarpieces, and other works of art are in need of urgent attention. Their rescue will require long and painstaking work, and help is greatly needed.

An international relief fund to stabilize and restore buildings and art works damaged in the earthquake has been established by the Friends of Assisi, together with the World Monuments Fund, a privately supported international preservation organization. As in 1966, in response to the flooding that devastated Venice, WMF will participate in the effort to save the priceless cultural heritage of Italy and to prevent further loss. WMF will work with the Italian authorities to identify a restoration project.

Your contribution will help in this vital effort to rescue and protect the precious treasures of the medieval heart of Italy. Please give generously.

World Monuments Fund/Assisi
949 Park Avenue
New York, NY 10028
Tel: (212) 517-9367
Fax: (212) 517-9494

World Monuments Fund/Assisi
39–40 St. James's Place
London, ENGLAND SW1A INS
Tel: (171) 499-8254
Fax: (171) 493-3982

Project Manager, English-language edition: Ellen Rosefsky Cohen
Editor, English-language edition: Elaine M. Stainton
Designer, English-language edition: Carol A. Robson

Library of Congress Catalog Card Number: 97–78102
ISBN 0–8109–2767–5 (pbk.)
ISBN 0–8109–4024–8 (bookclub hc.)

Originally published in Italy by Franco Cosimo Panini Editore
Photographs by Ghigo Roli
Copyright © 1997 Franco Cosimo Panini Editore
English translation copyright © 1998 Harry N. Abrams, Inc.

Harry N. Abrams, Inc.
100 Fifth Avenue
New York, N.Y. 10011
www.abramsbooks.com

Contents

Foreword

In the spring of 1999 the *Mirabilia Italiae* series, under the direction of Salvatore Settis, was to have released its ninth publication. This was to have been a two-volume set, consisting of a photographic atlas of the upper and lower basilicas of the Church of St. Francis in Assisi, and a volume of essays and entries, in Italian and English, edited by Giorgio Bonsanti. Professor Bonsanti is the director of the Opificio delle Pietre Dure in Florence, a fine arts restoration laboratory, and the author of a highly regarded monograph on Giotto.

A superb art photographer, Ghigo Roli, was engaged to provide a complete set of documentary photographs for the project. By chance, Mr. Roli was finishing his work in the upper basilica of the Church of St. Francis on the night of September 26, 1997, when the earthquake, now famous for its destruction of several parts of the church, struck. This powerful tremor shook the basilica so forcefully that two sections of the vaulting collapsed; it also weakened the structure of the rest of the building considerably. Miraculously, Mr. Roli and a number of others who were in the church that night escaped with their lives.

Fortunately, the photographs were not destroyed, but only slightly damaged. Tragically, however, the collapse killed two friars from the Order of St. Francis and two experts who had been sent by the Soprintendenza—the government office that oversees Italian cultural sites—to assess damages that had already been sustained in a smaller quake a few days earlier.

Despite our great sorrow at the loss of human life and the terrible damage to works of art important not only to Italian culture but to the artistic heritage of the world, we have decided to publish Mr. Roli's photographs, so that everyone who will be involved in saving and restoring the great frescoes of Cimabue and Giotto can see the paintings as they were.

For the present, we have had to suspend our work on the initial publication. We hope, however, that this book will allow the final photographs of the lost masterpieces of Assisi to be seen by art lovers throughout the world.

Franco Cosimo Panini

The Church
of St. Francis in Assisi

When we consider religious feeling and practice of the Middle Ages, we tend to think of it as solemn, and even gloomy, involving penitence and suffering. For St. Francis of Assisi, however, religion embodied joy. St. Francis recognized God in everything around him, including animals and other phenomena of nature. Thus he would call fire his "brother" and water his "sister"; he would confront a ferocious wolf and exhort it to become tame; and he would preach the word of God to birds alighting on the ground around him.

St. Francis was born in Assisi, a small town in the region of Umbria in central Italy, in 1182, the son of a rich wool merchant. After living a secular life as a young man (including a spell in prison after a battle), around 1205 he embraced a religious way of life with a strong inclination toward preaching. The desire to preach distinguished him from most of the monks of his century, who generally lived secluded lives in monasteries, from which they seldom emerged. In this respect, however, he was much like another great saint of his time, the Spaniard Dominic de Guzmán, founder of the Dominican order. While the Dominicans favored a learned, even intellectual, approach to religion, the Franciscans, by contrast, were thoroughly immersed in the life of the world and devoted to poverty (another of St. Francis's "sisters"). Indeed, St. Francis's desire to preach led him to travel great distances, even, according to his legend, to Egypt in 1219, where he tried to convert the sultan himself. Francis died on October 3, 1226. After his death two factions of his order took shape: the Spirituals, who wanted to keep themselves detached from the world, and the Conventuals, who were more involved in everyday life, and who eventually came to dominate the order.

St. Francis's influence in Italy was powerful indeed, and before long it extended abroad, especially to England, where the order was established as early as 1224. Immediately following Francis's death in 1226, construction began in Assisi on a church dedicated to him, which was to become the lower basilica of St. Francis. Two years after it was completed, work began on the upper church, for which the lower church acts as a foundation. The upper church was completed in 1236.

The lower church was built in the northern Italian Romanesque style, and is thus squat, broad, and barrel-vaulted. The upper church, however, was built in the Gothic style, which, although already well developed in France in the early thirteenth century, was new to Italy. The vaulting of the upper church, as in all Gothic buildings, rises in sections, called bays, to a height made possible by the use of pointed arches and a skeleton of columns and ribs. These ribs, which immediately support the vault, converge and intersect at the top of each bay. This skeletal construction, which is characteristic of Gothic architecture, relieves the walls of the immense weight of the stone roof, transferring it to the ribs, which in turn transfer it to the columns, from which it is carried to the church's floor. The columns, which stand against the walls of the nave—there are no side aisles in the upper church at Assisi—divide the space of the church into four bays. Each bay is cross-vaulted, that is, it is covered by a ribbed vault divided into four triangular sections. Between the nave and the apse is a transept, which is also cross-vaulted. Finally, the apse culminates in an elaborate presbytery, which contrasts with the more simple apsidal east end of the lower church.

As in the Gothic buildings of northern Europe, the ribbed structure that carries most of the weight of the roof at Assisi also allows the walls to be pierced by large windows. These are filled with multicolored stained glass, through which light can enter in abundance and illumi-nate the wall paintings, which were begun shortly after the church's completion.

Within a few decades, the walls of both the upper and lower churches were covered with frescoes. Such paintings were a very ancient tradition in Christian architecture, although cer-tain austere monastic orders, such as the Cistercians, had renounced them. The religious scenes portrayed on the walls of churches were not there for artistic expression, although we may be tempted to think of them in that way today. Rather, they were didactic. That is, their primary purpose was to provide the faithful, most of whom were unable to read, with easily recogniz-able and understandable illustrations of the stories of the Bible. Indeed, medieval fresco paint-ing of this type was called the "Bible of the Poor." We can easily imagine a priest addressing his congregation, gesturing toward the scenes from the Old and New Testaments on the wall as he derives some moral lesson from them, oblivious to the gulf between the realities of everyday life and those of the sacred texts to which we have become so accustomed in modern times. Throughout most of the Middle Ages, the need to have images available to illustrate a narra-tive could only be satisfied by painting cycles in public places, since there were so few books. Printed books would not become available at all until the fifteenth century, and not widely so until some time after that. Thus, when the basilicas of St. Francis were built, every book was a unique object, laboriously written and illustrated by hand, and therefore extremely expensive. Only very rich people, and community institutions, could afford to own them.

The frescoes in the lower basilica were begun around 1250; those in the upper basilica were begun around 1275. As in most churches in the Middle Ages, work began in the apse—at the east end of the church—and progressed gradually westward along the walls of the nave toward the inner wall of the façade. In the upper church, much of the painting was entrusted to a great Florentine artist, Cenni di Pepi, known as Cimabue. Cimabue painted the apse with frescoes illustrating the life of the Virgin, the left arm of the transept with a large Crucifixion and a cycle illustrating the Apocalypse of St. John, and the right arm of the transept with sto-ries from the legends of Sts. Peter and Paul, as well as another Crucifixion. Above Cimabue's frescoes in the right transept are some nearly illegible remnants of a painting of unknown authorship, possibly by a foreign (perhaps British) master, whose hand can also be detected in the better-preserved figures in the galleries of the same transept. In the left transept galleries there are figures by Cimabue, who is also responsible for the figures of the Four Evangelists in the sections of the ribbed vault over the transept crossing.

The state of preservation of all these works is poor, a fact that was already noted by the artist and biographer Giorgio Vasari in the mid-sixteenth century. The principal reason for the poor condition of these works is that they were painted *a secco*, that is, after the plaster on the wall had dried, a technique that is notoriously fragile. In true fresco painting (called in Italian *buon fresco*, or "good fresco"), the pigments are applied to wet plaster. As the plaster dries, a chemical transformation called "carbonation" takes place, which gives the painting such inter-nal cohesion that the colors are almost indestructible. They will last, in fact, as long as the plas-ter does. In painting applied *a secco*, however, the pigments do not bond with the plaster, and they are therefore considerably less durable. Moreover, Cimabue used a large amount of white lead in these paintings, which upon contact with the atmosphere is prone to oxidize and turn black. The result is an inversion of the relationships of depth and color. The very parts of the composition that were intended to be light, and thus project, turn dark and recede.

However, it is possible to perceive the qualities of Cimabue's painting even in its current state. His is a powerful, highly plastic art, and its volumes assume an emphatic sense of relief that conveys a strong dramatic impression. Cimabue still belongs to the ancient school of Byzantine painting, which has continued in some countries even to the present day. In the history of Italian painting, Cimabue marks the end of an era; by the time that he was painting, Giotto, who was destined to create a new manner of painting and with it change the course of Western art history, had already been born. Thus the historic position of Cimabue might, from this perspective, be compared to that of Johann Sebastian Bach in music.

Each of the Four Evangelists that Cimabue portrayed in the triangular sections of the vault is shown writing his Gospel. Each is identified by an inscription, and by the presence of his traditional symbol: Matthew by an angel, Mark by a lion, Luke by an ox, and John by an eagle. In front of each Evangelist stands a miniature city representing the part of the world to which he was sent to preach; these are identified by inscriptions: *Judea* for Matthew; *Ipanacchia* (Greece) for Luke; *Ytalia* for Mark; and *Asia* for John. While the portrayals of the other cities are entirely imaginary, the one that represents Italy features identifiable monuments specific to Rome: the Campidoglio (the Capitol Hill); the medieval Torre delle Milizie; the Church of St. John Lateran; the Castel Sant'Angelo (the tomb of Hadrian); and the rotunda of the Pantheon. This was an extraordinary innovation. For the first time since Antiquity, a new element was introduced into Western painting: the attempt to represent an actual place with topographical accuracy. The sections of the vault that contain the figures of the Evangelists are bordered with a variety of decorative motifs. These include heads and plant forms, which arise from large vases supported by cherubs that could be called, in accordance with the tradition of Greek art, "telamons," or figures designated to bear a weight.

The decoration of the nave continued, moving from the transept crossing toward the inner wall of the façade. For the work on the upper walls, Cimabue was replaced by other artists. These painters probably came from Rome, where, according to surviving documents, the most important studios were those of Filippo Rusuti and the Franciscan painter Jacopo Torriti, to whom art historians have attributed the greater part of the scenes in the upper nave. These scenes include a Genesis cycle on the highest part of the wall, and incidents from the life of Christ in the middle section. On the lower section, which starts at the east end of the right-hand wall, progresses westward to the inner wall of the façade, and then continues back toward the altar (thus in a U-shape), is the famous cycle of episodes from the life of St. Francis, which is traditionally attributed to the school of Giotto.

The vault of the bay nearest the altar is painted blue and dotted with golden stars. The vault of the next bay—that is, the third bay from the façade and the third from the altar—features four tondi (circles), one in each section, each enclosing an image: Christ the Redeemer (facing the entrance), the Virgin, St. Francis, and St. John the Baptist. Each tondo is flanked by two large angels. Depicted in the triangles formed by the ribs, where each section of the vault rises from the nave columns, are figures of standing nude cherubs. Deriving as they do from pagan Classical art, these figures seem somewhat incongruous from an iconographic point of view, but they are an understandable motif from the hand of a Roman artist such as Torriti.

The next vault (over the second bay from the entrance) is decorated, like the one near the altar, with a starry sky. Here the blue pigment, which was derived from copper, has turned green in some spots from humidity; chemically speaking, azurite has turned to malachite. Lastly, next to the internal wall of the façade, is another vault filled with frescoes of figures. These represent the Doctors of the Church—the great early Christian theologians whose writings laid the foundations of Church doctrine. Thus we see St. Jerome, who translated the books of the Bible from Greek and Hebrew into the Latin Vulgate, so called because it thus became accessible to a much broader readership, just as Martin Luther, centuries later, would translate it into German. Born near Aquilea, in the Veneto, around 347, Jerome left Rome to live as a hermit in the Near East, where he died, in Jerusalem, in 420. We also see St. Gregory the Great, the pope who lived from 540 to around 604 and made a number of important decisions increasing the autonomy of the Church. In the third section sits St. Augustine, who was born in Numidia (present-day Algeria) in 354 and died at Hippo (now Annaba), where he was bishop, in 430. Augustine's *Confessions* are one of the first texts in the history of world literature in which one may read an account of the journey of an individual's soul toward a knowledge of God. On the Saturday before Easter in 367, Augustine was baptized by St. Ambrose, the fourth Doctor of the Church, who was born at Treviri before 340 and died in Milan, where he was bishop, in 397.

Augustine and Gregory are shown dictating their books to a deacon; Jerome and Ambrose are shown reading. Seated before Jerome and Ambrose are, respectively, a monk (Jerome, we recall, lived in the desert), and another deacon, also both reading. The paintings are bordered by a rich decoration of geometrical, floral, and foliate motifs; as in the other decorated vaults, cherubs stand at the corners of each section. On the interior curve of the arch just inside the entrance are figures of saints, including St. Francis, St. Clare (the founder of the Poor Clares, the female branch of the Franciscans), and the ancient patron of Assisi, St. Rufinus.

After seeing the poor state of conservation of the earlier vault paintings, one is struck by the brilliant color and convincing evocation of space in these splendid images. The feeling of space is infinitely more complex than in those earlier works, and it relates these scenes to the paintings on the walls, which, beginning with two events from the life of Isaac and continuing through a series of episodes from the New Testament, lead to the legend of St. Francis.

The paintings of the Four Doctors are characterized by a precise sense of their pictorial space, which seems to be endowed with a presence of its own, independent of the figures occupying it. This, of course, is the one of the dominant features of Giotto's revolutionary approach to representation, and one of his most important contributions to Western painting.

Giotto was born in the environs of Florence around 1267 and died in January 1337. In the words of an artist of the early fifteenth century, Giotto "transformed painting from Greek into Latin, and adapted it to modern use." In other words, he abandoned the rigid conventions of Byzantine painting, transforming it into a living language that his contemporaries felt they could use with fluent proficiency. Giotto's figures appear to have real volume, and to occupy real, three-dimensional space; moreover, their gestures and expressions communicate recognizable meanings. Using these devices, Giotto discovered how to narrate a story rich in human feeling, and how to represent actions and emotions with a hitherto unknown clarity. The images of the Four Doctors of the Church must surely be attributed to Giotto, although he would have had the customary assistance of a number of collaborators. The frescoes can probably be dated around 1288.

The three decorated vaults in the upper church contain, starting from the entrance: the Four Doctors, that is, the four great theologians of the church, the founders of its doctrine and discipline; these are followed by the four great Intercessors, that is, Christ, the Virgin, and Francis and John the Baptist, two saints dedicated to praying for the faithful; and finally, the Four Evangelists, the witnesses to the life and teachings of Christ on earth. Anyone entering the basilica was expected to turn his gaze upward toward these images, as if toward heavenly windows opening to reveal the cornerstones of faith and catechism. The church's columns, which rise in a continuous line to the ribs, which rise again to meet in a kind of nucleus at the apex of the vault of each bay, were intended to direct the believer's eyes to these "windows" with the precision of a railroad track.

As of this writing, the extraordinary view down the nave of the upper basilica of Assisi, which had hardly changed over the centuries, has now been tragically altered. Suddenly the tranquil existence of the basilica, visited each year by millions of pilgrims coming to seek the origins of the Franciscan message, has been thrown into disarray. The earthquake has reminded us once again of the precariousness of human life, institutions, and creations. The shock took the lives of four people inside the church, which for 670 years had welcomed pilgrims with paintings of religious stories on its walls. Of the many damages caused by the earthquake to the works of art in the basilica and the monastery, the most devastating by far was the irreparable destruction of one of Cimabue's Evangelists, the figure of St. Matthew, and of one of Giotto's Four Doctors (St. Jerome), and the black-robed monk assisting him. Other figures and decorative elements were also destroyed. Suddenly our knowledge of these works has been consigned exclusively to photographs and to memory. Consciously, we experience this violent change as an intolerable affront, for art transcends the mere individual; it belongs to all of humanity, and every one of its expressions belongs to all of us personally. We must certainly shed tears, on this sorrowful occasion, for the two friars and the two experts killed in the collapse of the basilica. But we must also weep for the works of Cimabue and Giotto, which are gone forever. We feel this tragedy even more keenly because the Church of St. Francis is one of the principal sites of the Catholic faith, and one of the cornerstones of Christianity. It has always been a miracle, at once divine and human, that faith and art could come together as they do in the basilica of Assisi.

Giorgio Bonsanti

Assisi, The Earthquake of September 26, 1997

By now I feel like one of the family, here in the upper basilica. I've already been working some four months on my photographic survey. It's an ambitious project: two thousand photos that will eventually document the basilica's entire artistic treasure.

I spent nearly every night of the past summer photographing, episode by episode, this great artistic story.

More than once it occurred to me that perhaps, in some small way, all this had been made just for me—for my eyes and for my mind.

Thursday, September 4, 12:10 a.m.

I am on the second level from the top of my scaffolding, some 12.5 meters (about 41 feet) above the ground. I am finishing up photographing the details of the saints in the inner curve of the great arch of the first bay, just above the left-hand lancet window. The final notes of the Bach I was listening to died out just a short while ago: there is total silence. I hear a dull rumbling from the east-northeast. A half hour earlier, when I went outside to smoke a cigarette, the sky was calm and starry: it couldn't be a storm. The rumbling becomes a subterranean thunder. I realize it is an earthquake. I have barely the time to set down the light meter, sit down on the case of my Sinar camera, and grab the railing. The thunder rapidly approaches. It enters the Basilica, which becomes a giant resonance-box, and turns it into a roar. The scaffolding vibrates and rattles a long time, but holds up in the end. A few chips fall from the walls, then the silence returns. Several minutes later, Father Cosma arrives, to see if everything is all right. I'm unconcerned; the basilica has been standing for eight hundred years, I think to myself, it's not going to choose this very moment to fall. I resume my work. I finish the series of fourteen saints, and at 4:30 a.m. I go to sleep. The earthquake registered "six" on the Richter scale, say the papers the next day, with the epicenter at Colfiorito.

Friday, September 26, shortly after midnight

After two nights spent shooting general views of Cimabue's scenes in the transept, I begin tackling the details. I encounter an obstacle to the first shot: the rope to the bell next to the sacristy door partially covers the fresco. I take the key, go outside, and, circling around the apse, open the old lock to the turret that leads to the attic. I stop after the first sixty-two steps of the narrow, monolithic spiral staircase that I have scaled so many times I can do it in the dark. I open the little door leading to the gallery—a walkway 7.5 meters high (about 24½ feet) and barely half a meter wide, which runs along the interior perimeter of the basilica, above the Giotto and Cimabue cycles, at the point where the walls become narrower. I've used it several times before to position my lights, and I know every nook and cranny of it, every electrical cable, every obstacle. In the apse area this walkway is covered by arcades where, usually, I am startled by the sudden flight of a dozen or so bats living there. Not tonight, however. Thinking over the evening, I realize that I didn't see even one of these customary companions of mine. I go back, in my mind, to seven o'clock, when the church closes and I usually turn off all the lights and turn on only my floodlights, which attract large quantities of insects. But no bats tonight. It's the first time in four months. Thinking back on the tremor of September 4, I don't recall seeing them that evening, either. There's going to be another shock, I think to myself, convinced of the Basilica's solidity and confident of my scaffolding's ability to pass another test. I remove the bell rope, go back downstairs, close up, and go back inside the basilica to continue my work.

2:30 a.m.

I've just finished shooting the last three frames of the south wall of the transept, five details, the last of which shows a group of people with a large, ancient, stucco-filled crack running through them. I am 7 meters (23 feet) above the ground. I turn off my floods; there's just a small lamp still shining over my head. I study the proofs of the book and look at my ladder, trying to decide what needs to be done next. I'm missing a detail of the eleventh frame and have to move the scaffolding to the north side of the transept. I put on Beethoven's "Emperor" concerto and get ready to descend the scaffolding.

2:33 a.m.

There's the thunder again. It's stronger and faster this time; or perhaps I didn't hear the first rumbling over the sound of the music. Already sitting down, I grab the railing, cradle my head between my shoulders. The thunder explodes into the basilica, lifting it up and dropping it, shaking it throughout. My scaffolding rattles like a toy. The aluminum joints creak nonstop. I look over at my equipment bench, the electrical generators, the floodlights; everything is bound together with thin cords: they will collapse all together, or not at all. The thunder seems to be receding when suddenly I hear an even louder din, similar to that of hail against the roof of a car: it's all the chips from the walls and vaults raining down on the floor, seemingly endlessly, echoing inside the deserted church.

Then silence, broken only by the notes of my Beethoven.

This was serious, this time, I thought. I descend from the scaffolding in the semidarkness, enter the sacristy, turn on all the lights in the church and go back to have a look. The sky of the vaults is full of clouds of white dust; at various points streams of sand are still falling; the floor is covered with the white of the dust and the red, blue, and green of the frescoed plaster. I want to cry.

2:40 a.m.

I take a large, battery-powered beacon I usually use to illuminate the corners of the most critical frames or to examine remote details, and I begin to study the damage. I take care not to step on the fragments of fresco on the floor. I look with shock at every crack, every white hole in the frescoed ceiling. I can't decide whether I should go outside or not. It is as though those walls are the walls of my house, as if those inexplicable wounds are on my own skin. I begin examining everything carefully. The last Cimabue I photographed has white holes, but fortunately they're in the ancient plastering; menacing cracks run along the ribs at the juncture with the vaults. A white fissure in the archivolt of the interior façade cuts diagonally through *St. Francis and St. Clare*. There is a continuous crack in the great arch of the south façade of the transept along the line where it abuts the vault. The vault itself, directly above my scaffolding, has large white fissures running through the starry sky. In the north arm of the transept there is a large piece of stone near a hole in the flooring. I look above, unable to figure out where it came from. I look at it more closely: its hexagonal shape is familiar. I must have seen it somewhere from very close up, perhaps touched it—but of course, it's the column of the double lancet. I illuminate the great stained-glass window; halfway up, at the point where the left column is crossed by a metal tie beam, a segment is missing, the very piece now at my feet. I pick it up; it must weigh 15 to 18 pounds. I look more closely at its place, measuring in steps the distance from the wall. The hole in the flooring is in the very spot where I was supposed to position myself. But for a difference of two minutes, I would have been right there.

3:00 a.m., approximately

Strangely, no one has come up to the church yet. I go down into the cloister. A roar of water rushing into the courtyard has drawn the attention of some friars, who are trying to figure out where it is coming from. A pipe has burst, but we don't know where. There are a few more light tremors. Then we go up together into the upper basilica. They had not imagined that the damage would be so great. I illumine the wounds with my beacon; on their faces I see the same bewildered pain I had felt myself a short while ago. Father Giulio, Keeper of the Sacred Convent, also arrives, followed by Sergio Fusetti, chief conservator of the Basilica, and a few novice monks. We begin gathering up the largest fragments to keep them from getting stepped on, and we arrange them in order on the benches. I should finish photographing, but I only want to go outside to see the stars again. First, however, I must take care of my scaffolding. My mind fills with images of churches I'd seen in Irpinia [near Naples] after the 1981 earthquake, of which only the apses were saved. I move the scaffolding right in front of the papal throne, leaving all the equipment on top. Father Giulio invites me for a cup of coffee.

Around 4:00 a.m.

In a common room of the monastery, we drink coffee, trading impressions. A few more tremors. Father Giulio decides to close the basilica to visitors. Nobody objects. Things need to be inspected.

I go outside to smoke a cigarette. I don't feel sleepy. I don't fall asleep until after six o'clock.

8:45 a.m.

It's a clear, warm, late-summer morning. Cappuccino, brioche, a glance at the newspaper. In a few days, in any case, I would have had to dismantle the scaffolding to allow free passage in the basilica for the feast of its patron saint on October 4. I feel tired and worried. I decide to pack up early and go back home. I will continue the work in November. I enter the church to start the dismantling. There are journalists, photographers, TV cameramen. Someone asks me to pose for a photo showing the plaster chips that had fallen during the night. The friars come and go. Sergio Fusetti has his restorers climb up a small scaffolding, where they begin to assess the condition of the St. Francis cycle, tapping the plaster to see if it has come loose at any points. The technical experts from the Soprintendenza arrive. With my torch I show them the highest cracks, which are hard to see, and the most serious damage. They draft their report. The tremors continue, now soft, now stronger. We're not concerned; everyone thinks they're aftershocks.

Around 10:20 a.m.

I remember the bell rope I left on the gallery. I retrace my steps of the night before. I open the door to the stairway, pass through the apse arcades; the bats still haven't returned. I think there are going to be still more aftershocks. I put the bell rope back to where it was. On the stairs I run into Father Lucanio and Maurizio, one of the church guards. Together we go up to the second order of arcades, to have a closer look at the vault; the people down below, inside the basilica, look tiny. Then we go farther up still, to the attic, one great room as large as the entire basilica. We walk over the whole vault as far as the small rose window of the façade. Over this last stretch there are three long, parallel cracks marking the vertex of the exterior curve of the arch below. We retrace our steps. In the area above the transept I see, leaning against a vault, a large, cross-shaped key, used perhaps to tighten the catenaries linking the outside walls. We go back down into the basilica. More tremors. I climb up my scaffolding, which is still in the apse, to begin, finally, to dismantle it. It is past eleven o'clock. No use; I'm wanted on the telephone. I have a long conversation about work. The line gets cut off. They call back.

11:40 a.m.

Sergio Fusetti is looking for me, because he needs my floodlight to examine the frescoes with a close-range light. I climb down from the scaffolding. We are still talking about damages as we move toward the entrance.

11:41 a.m.

I leave the light with one of the boys who work for Sergio. I want a cigarette, and I head toward the main portal, to go outside.

11:42 a.m.

I have one foot still in the church and one already outside when I hear the thunder return. "There it is again!" I call out loud, to warn the two restorers who are removing paint from the large wooden door next to the one through which I am exiting. In the corner of my eye I see the jambs of the portal rise as the thunder explodes in a roar, then fall back down, lurching first forward then back; I step away, then look up. Now the whole façade is shaking, vibrating; the large scaffold used for restorations on the façade rattles, trembles, jumps. There is a workman at the top of it; here too, they had been dismantling in preparation for the feast of St. Francis. The worker's face twists into silent grimaces. He is holding a long iron beam in his hands, which he was about to lower with a pulley; he obviously would like to throw it over so he could grab onto something. But there are seven or eight of us below; fortunately, he manages to hang on to it; like a dancer caught off step, he stumbles forward and back to keep his balance.

Then just as it came, the thunder fades. The very heavy door through which I exited is now closed. Through a crack, a dense cloud of ocher-colored dust escapes. I realize that this time, something more than paint chips has fallen. I approach, try pushing the door open, but it is blocked by rubble. I hear voices calling inside. The other door is still open, kept ajar by a small scaffold that was half in and half out, and whose metal platform has saved the two restorers who were directly under it. But the entrance is blocked by rubble and by the twisted iron rods of the large glass inner door, which has been pulverized. People keep calling from inside. I still have the key to the rear door in my pocket. I run around the church, across the courtyard, and up the staircase leading to the transept. The door is half-closed; I go in. There is total darkness. There has been a power failure, and a thick, irrespirable dust cloud envelops everything. I have a small electric flashlight, which I turn on. I can hardly see the ends of my own shoes. A dust white silhouette appears. We head toward the door and throw it open. He has a camera with a flash, and we go back inside, as far as a large pile of rubble where the altar once stood. Together, he with his flash and I with my flashlight, we try to get people's attention, to point them to the exit. White, dumbfounded phantoms begin to emerge; the first has a large television camera; he is the cameraman who filmed the collapse live. I count seven more people. I have trouble breathing; I don't hear any more cries. At my feet I see the large key I'd seen a short while before in the attic. The vault has fallen. Unable to breathe any longer, I run outside. In my mind I count again the number of people inside the church: twenty-two, perhaps twenty-five. Putting the rubble I saw at the entrance together with that which I saw in the transept, I imagine the worst: a single, great collapse. Only in the afternoon will I learn that only three sections of the vault have collapsed. Almost everyone got out through the façade entrance while I was in the transept. Still missing were the two experts from the Soprintendenza and two friars.

In the afternoon, I meet the restorer with whom I'd left my light. We embrace; he was under the fallen vault with three other young men. When the rumbling began, he aimed the lamp up at the ceiling, and they just barely managed to step aside in time, huddling up against the wall.

October 15

Writing these lines, I recall that even last night, around 2:30 a.m., I woke up with a start. Every night I see those same images of chaos, superimposed and very clear: the scaffolding banging against the façade; the darkness inside the basilica from which, around the piles of rubble, confused white phantoms appear; the large key on the floor, and then the great door that won't open, with people calling and running and weeping, the great, immobile church trembling, the rents in the vaulting, the rubble lined up on the lawn outside, the work of the firemen, the dogs and the nurses, and then the great cloud of ocher dust, filmed live as it snuffs out, without distinction, the lives of four people, the symbol of a faith, and a treasury of art.

Ghigo Roli

The Vault of the Upper Church

1

2

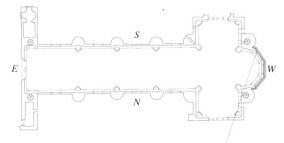

2

1 On pages 20 and 21, the complex of
basilicas of St. Francis of Assisi, seen from
the southeast (Scala photo)

2 The apse of the upper church, seen from
the fifteenth-century cloister (Scala photo)

3

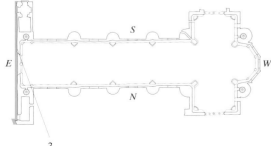

3 The façade of the upper basilica

3

The Upper Basilica
Iconographic Plan

The decoration of the lower church of St. Francis began around 1250. That of the upper church began around 1275, starting from the apse, and was entrusted to Cimabue. He provided the apse with scenes from the life of the Virgin, which were fortunately not damaged by the earthquake and are thus not reproduced in the iconographic diagram. In the left transept, Cimabue painted a cycle from the Apocalypse of St. John and a marvelous Crucifixion; in the right transept, he depicted the martyrdoms of Sts. Peter and Paul and another beautiful Crucifixion; and in the central vault of the eastern side of the crossing, he portrayed the four Evangelists, accompanied by highly innovative representations of cities symbolizing the places where each of them preached (partially destroyed).

The decoration was continued along the nave walls, probably by Roman masters, who painted the Biblical events portrayed on the northern wall and the episodes from the life of Christ on the southern wall. This same group of Roman painters was probably also responsible for the vault fresco of the Intercessors: Christ, the Virgin, St. John the Baptist, and St. Francis.

The episodes from the life of St. Francis, which cover the entire lower section of the nave starting from the far end of the right-hand wall, have traditionally been attributed to Giotto and his assistants.

These same artists were also responsible for the saints on the archivolt of the inner façade (for the most part destroyed), and for the vault containing the depictions of the Doctors of the Church, one section of which collapsed in the earthquake.

Transept and Nave

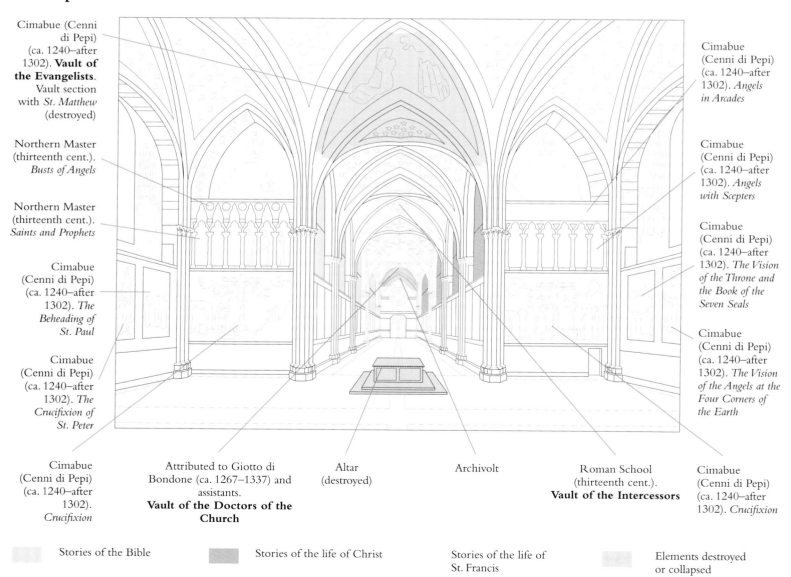

Cimabue (Cenni di Pepi) (ca. 1240–after 1302). **Vault of the Evangelists**. Vault section with *St. Matthew* (destroyed)

Northern Master (thirteenth cent.). *Busts of Angels*

Northern Master (thirteenth cent.). *Saints and Prophets*

Cimabue (Cenni di Pepi) (ca. 1240–after 1302). *The Beheading of St. Paul*

Cimabue (Cenni di Pepi) (ca. 1240–after 1302). *The Crucifixion of St. Peter*

Cimabue (Cenni di Pepi) (ca. 1240–after 1302). *Angels in Arcades*

Cimabue (Cenni di Pepi) (ca. 1240–after 1302). *Angels with Scepters*

Cimabue (Cenni di Pepi) (ca. 1240–after 1302). *The Vision of the Throne and the Book of the Seven Seals*

Cimabue (Cenni di Pepi) (ca. 1240–after 1302). *The Vision of the Angels at the Four Corners of the Earth*

Cimabue (Cenni di Pepi) (ca. 1240–after 1302). *Crucifixion*

Attributed to Giotto di Bondone (ca. 1267–1337) and assistants. **Vault of the Doctors of the Church**

Altar (destroyed)

Archivolt

Roman School (thirteenth cent.). **Vault of the Intercessors**

Cimabue (Cenni di Pepi) (ca. 1240–after 1302). *Crucifixion*

Stories of the Bible

Stories of the life of Christ

Stories of the life of St. Francis

Elements destroyed or collapsed

Inner Façade

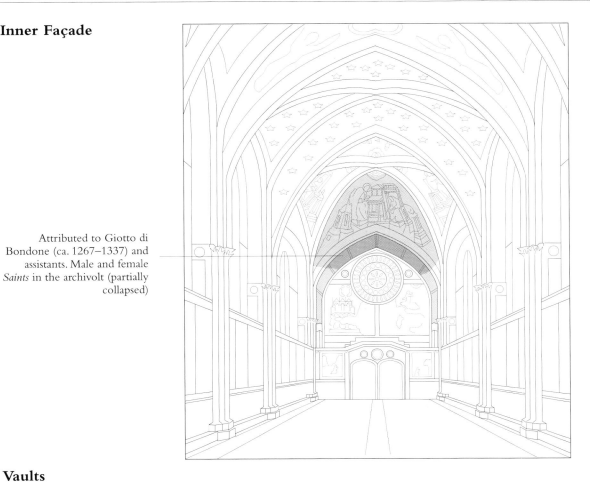

Attributed to Giotto di Bondone (ca. 1267–1337) and assistants. Male and female *Saints* in the archivolt (partially collapsed)

Vaults

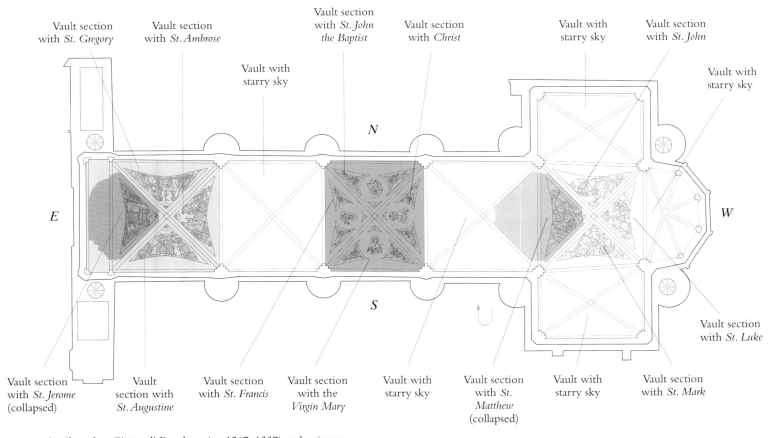

Vault section with *St. Gregory*

Vault section with *St. Ambrose*

Vault with starry sky

Vault section with *St. John the Baptist*

Vault section with *Christ*

Vault with starry sky

Vault section with *St. John*

Vault with starry sky

N

E

S

W

Vault section with *St. Luke*

Vault section with *St. Jerome* (collapsed)

Vault section with *St. Augustine*

Vault section with *St. Francis*

Vault section with the *Virgin Mary*

Vault with starry sky

Vault section with *St. Matthew* (collapsed)

Vault with starry sky

Vault section with *St. Mark*

Attributed to Giotto di Bondone (ca. 1267–1337) and assistants
Vault of the Doctors of the Church

Roman School (thirteenth cent.)
Vault of the Intercessors

Cimabue (Cenni di Pepi) (ca. 1240–after 1302)
Vault of the Evangelists

4

5

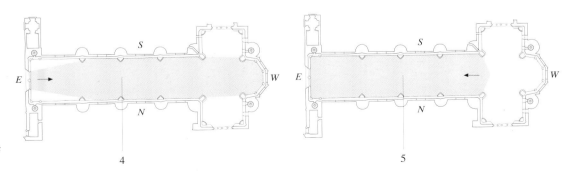

4 View of the nave from the inner façade
5 View of the nave from the transept

4

5

6 View of the nave from the apse

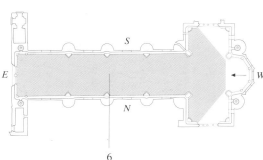

Archivolt of the Inner Façade
Iconographic Plan

On the archivolt of the inner façade are eight pairs of male and female saints, some of them unrecognizable.

Among the more outstanding of these pairings are the *St. Francis and St. Clare* and the *St. Benedict and St. Anthony*, which unfortunately collapsed in the earthquake.

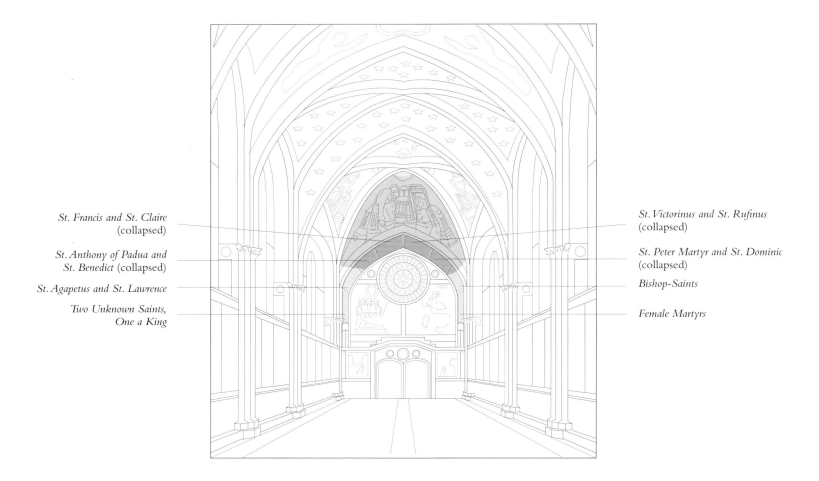

St. Francis and St. Claire
(collapsed)

St. Anthony of Padua and St. Benedict (collapsed)

St. Agapetus and St. Lawrence

Two Unknown Saints, One a King

St. Victorinus and St. Rufinus
(collapsed)

St. Peter Martyr and St. Dominic
(collapsed)

Bishop-Saints

Female Martyrs

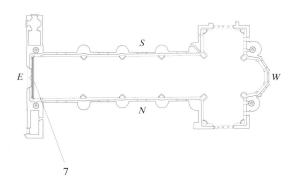

7 Inner façade (Ciol photo)

7

8

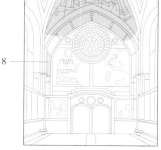

Interior façade
Inner arch of the archivolt

Attributed to Giotto di Bondone (ca. 1267–1337) and assistants
8 *Two Unknown Saints, One a King*

9

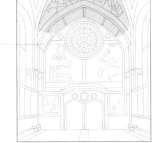

9

Interior façade
Inner arch of the archivolt

Attributed to Giotto di Bondone (ca. 1267–1337) and assistants
9 *St. Agapetus and St. Lawrence*

10

Interior façade
Inner arch of the archivolt

Attributed to Giotto di Bondone (ca. 1267–1337) and assistants
10 *St. Anthony of Padua and St. Benedict*
(destroyed)

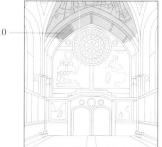

11

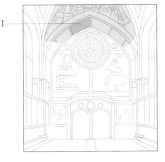

11

Interior façade
Inner arch of the archivolt

Attributed to Giotto di Bondone (ca. 1267–1337) and assistants
11 *St. Francis and St. Clare* (destroyed)

12

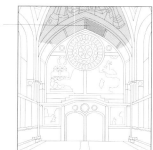

12

Interior façade
Inner arch of the archivolt

Attributed to Giotto di Bondone (ca. 1267–1337) and assistants
12 *St. Victorinus and St. Rufinus* (destroyed)

13

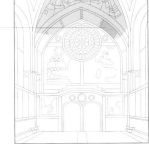

13

Interior façade
Inner arch of the archivolt

Attributed to Giotto di Bondone (ca. 1267–1337) and assistants
13 *St. Peter Martyr and St. Dominic* (destroyed)

14

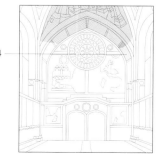

14

Interior façade
Inner arch of the archivolt

Attributed to Giotto di Bondone (ca. 1267–1337) and assistants
14 *Bishop-Saints*

15

15

Interior façade
Inner arch of the archivolt

Attributed to Giotto di Bondone (ca. 1267–1337) and assistants
15 *Female Martyrs*

Interior façade
Inner arch of the archivolt

Attributed to Giotto di Bondone
(ca. 1267–1337) and assistants
16 *St. Francis*, detail (destroyed)

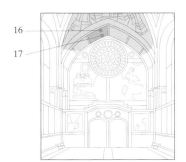

16

17

Interior façade
Inner arch of the archivolt

Attributed to Giotto di Bondone
(ca. 1267–1337) and assistants
17 *St. Clare*, detail (destroyed)

Vault of the Doctors of the Church
Iconographic Plan

In the sections of the vault adjacent to the internal façade of the basilica (the first vault upon entering), Giotto painted in fresco the Doctors of the Church, each of whom is identified by an inscription beneath the cloud above his head, which supports an image of the Redeemer. We thus recognize St. Jerome, St. Augustine, St. Ambrose, and St. Gregory. Jerome and Ambrose are shown reading, in the company of a monk and a deacon, respectively; the others are shown dictating their books to a deacon.

All of these figures are placed in a complex architectural setting of aediculae, thrones, and lecterns adorned with twisted columns and rich inlay.

The earthquakes that struck central Italy caused the collapse of the vault section containing the fresco of *St. Jerome*, destroying not only his figure, but that of the black-robed monk accompanying him, and many decorative motifs.

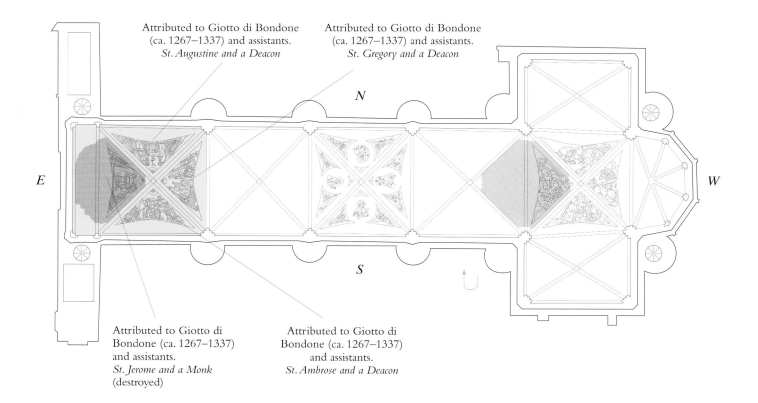

Attributed to Giotto di Bondone
(ca. 1267–1337) and assistants.
St. Augustine and a Deacon

Attributed to Giotto di Bondone
(ca. 1267–1337) and assistants.
St. Gregory and a Deacon

N

E

W

S

Attributed to Giotto di
Bondone (ca. 1267–1337)
and assistants.
St. Jerome and a Monk
(destroyed)

Attributed to Giotto di
Bondone (ca. 1267–1337)
and assistants.
St. Ambrose and a Deacon

Attributed to Giotto di Bondone
(ca. 1267–1337) and assistants.
St. Augustine and a Deacon

Attributed to
Giotto di
Bondone
(ca. 1267–1337)
and assistants.
*St. Jerome and a
Monk* (destroyed)

Attributed to
Giotto di
Bondone
(ca. 1267–1337)
and assistants.
*St. Gregory and
a Deacon*

Attributed to Giotto di Bondone
(ca. 1267–1337) and assistants.
St. Ambrose and a Deacon

Attributed to Giotto di Bondone
(ca. 1267–1337) and assistants
18 The vault of the Doctors of the Church

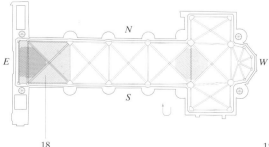

Vault of the Doctors of the Church

Attributed to Giotto di Bondone
(ca. 1267–1337) and assistants
19 Vault section with *St. Jerome and a Monk*
(destroyed)

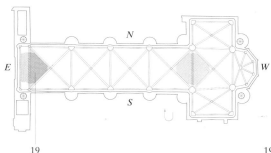

19

19

20

Vault of the Doctors of the Church
Vault section with *St. Jerome and a Monk*
(destroyed)

Attributed to Giotto di Bondone
(ca. 1267–1337) and assistants
20 *St. Jerome*

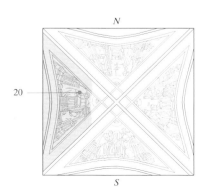

21

Vault of the Doctors of the Church
Vault section with *St. Jerome and a Monk* (destroyed)

Attributed to Giotto di Bondone (ca. 1267–1337) and assistants
21 *Monk Reading*

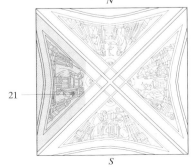

Vault of the Doctors of the Church

Attributed to Giotto di Bondone
(ca. 1267–1337) and assistants
22 Vault section with *St. Ambrose and a
Deacon*

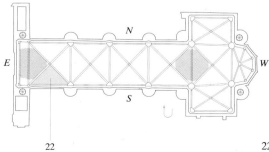

22

22

Vault of the Doctors of the Church
Vault section with *St. Ambrose and a Deacon*

Attributed to Giotto di Bondone
(ca. 1267–1337) and assistants
23 *St. Ambrose*

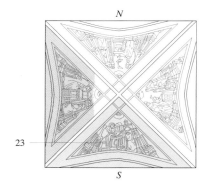

23

24

Vault of the Doctors of the Church
Vault section with *St. Ambrose and a Deacon*

Attributed to Giotto di Bondone (ca. 1267–1337) and assistants
24 *Deacon Reading*

Vault of the Doctors of the Church

Attributed to Giotto di Bondone
(ca. 1267–1337) and assistants

25 Vault section with *St. Gregory and a Deacon*

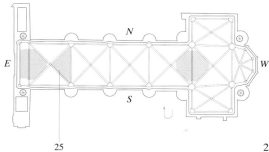

25

25

S·GREGORIVS DOCTOR·

S·AVGVSTINV DOCTOR·

26

Vault of the Doctors of the Church
Vault section with *St. Gregory and a Deacon*

Attributed to Giotto di Bondone
(ca. 1267–1337) and assistants
26 *St. Gregory*

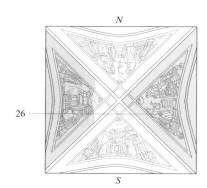

27

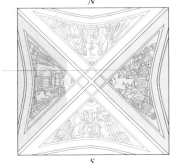

Vault of the Doctors of the Church
Vault section with *St. Gregory and a Deacon*

Attributed to Giotto di Bondone (ca. 1267–1337) and assistants
27 *Deacon Writing from Dictation*

Vault of the Doctors of the Church

Attributed to Giotto di Bondone
(ca. 1267–1337) and assistants

28 Vault section with *St. Augustine and a
Deacon*

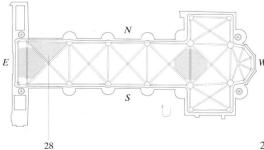

28

28

S·AGVSTINVS
DOCTOR·

Vault of the Doctors of the Church
Vault section with *St. Augustine and a Deacon*

Attributed to Giotto di Bondone
(ca. 1267–1337) and assistants
29 *St. Augustine*

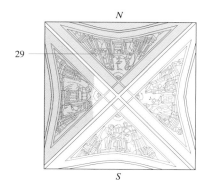

29

30

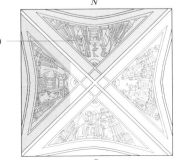

Vault of the Doctors of the Church
Vault section with *St. Augustine and a Deacon*

Attributed to Giotto di Bondone (ca. 1267–1337) and assistants
30 *Deacon Writing from Dictation*

Vault of the Four Intercessors
Iconographic Plan

The vault of the central bay of the basilica (the third from the entrance as well as from the altar) is divided into four triangular sections, each of which contains a fresco of one of the Four Intercessors. These Intercessors, who can obtain salvation for the faithful with their prayers, are Christ, the Virgin, St. John the Baptist, and St. Francis.

The work of artists from the Roman schools of Filippo Rusuti and Jacopo Torriti, these four figures are inscribed within tondi (circles), each of which is flanked by a pair of angels. In the triangular areas at the base of the vault segment are naked cherubs, derived from Classical sources. This is the only one of the frescoed vaults that was essentially spared destruction by the quake.

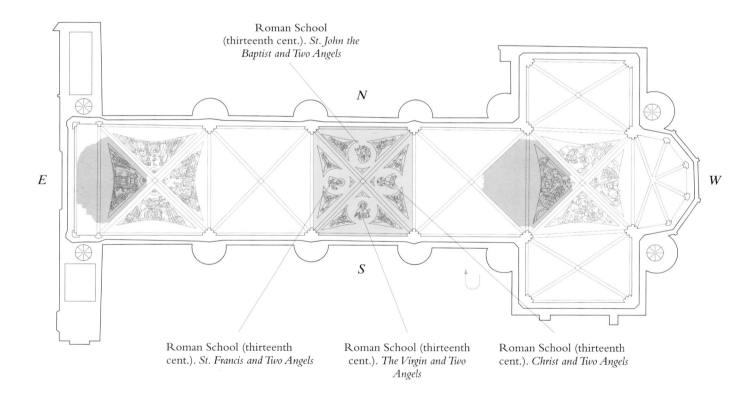

Roman School (thirteenth cent.). *St. John the Baptist and Two Angels*

Roman School (thirteenth cent.). *St. Francis and Two Angels*

Roman School (thirteenth cent.). *The Virgin and Two Angels*

Roman School (thirteenth cent.). *Christ and Two Angels*

Roman School (thirteenth cent.)
31 Vault of the Intercessors

32

Vault of the Intercessors

Roman School (thirteenth cent.)

32 Vault section with *The Virgin and Two Angels*

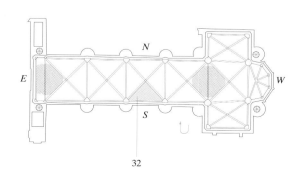

32

33

Vault of the Intercessors

Roman School (thirteenth cent.)

33 Vault section with *Christ and Two Angels*

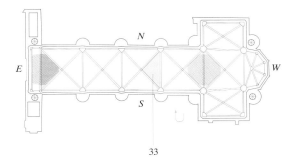

33

34

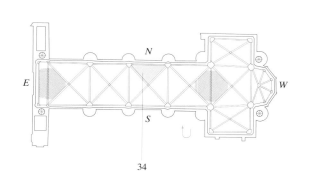

Vault of the Intercessors

Roman School (thirteenth cent.)

34 Vault section with *St. John the Baptist and Two Angels*

34

35

Vault of the Intercessors

Roman School (thirteenth cent.)
35 Vault section with *St. Francis
and Two Angels*

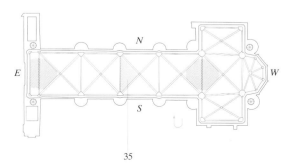

35

36

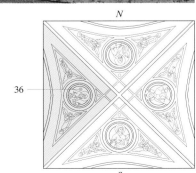

Vault of the Intercessors
Vault section with *St. Francis and Two Angels*

Roman School (thirteenth cent.)
36 *St. Francis*

37

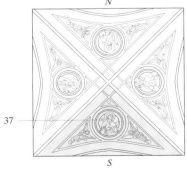

Vault of the Intercessors
Vault section with *The Virgin and Two Angels*

Roman School (thirteenth cent.)
37 *The Virgin*

38

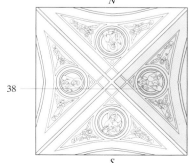

Vault of the Intercessors
Vault section with *Christ and Two Angels*
Roman School (thirteenth cent.)
38 *Christ*

39

Vault of the Intercessors
Vault section with *St. John the Baptist
and Two Angels*

Roman School (thirteenth cent.)
39 *St. John the Baptist*

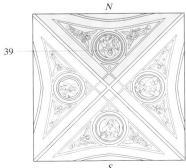

Vault of the Evangelists
Iconographic Plan

In the four sections of the crossing vault, Cimabue painted, against a gold background, the four Evangelists, each with his traditional symbol and the country where he preached the Gospel, represented by a city. Thus Matthew is accompanied by the angel and by *Judea*; Mark by the lion and by *Ytalia*; Luke by the ox and by *Ipanacchia* (Greece); John by the eagle and by *Asia*.

The cities here depicted are entirely imaginary except for the one representing Italy, which is clearly identifiable as Rome. In it, one may recognize such monuments as the Campidoglio (the Capitol Hill), the medieval Torre delle Milizie, the Church of St. John Lateran, the Castel Sant'Angelo (the round tomb of Hadrian), and the domed Pantheon. The quake that struck the basilica caused the almost complete collapse of the vault section decorated with the image of St. Matthew. Only a few fragments still remain.

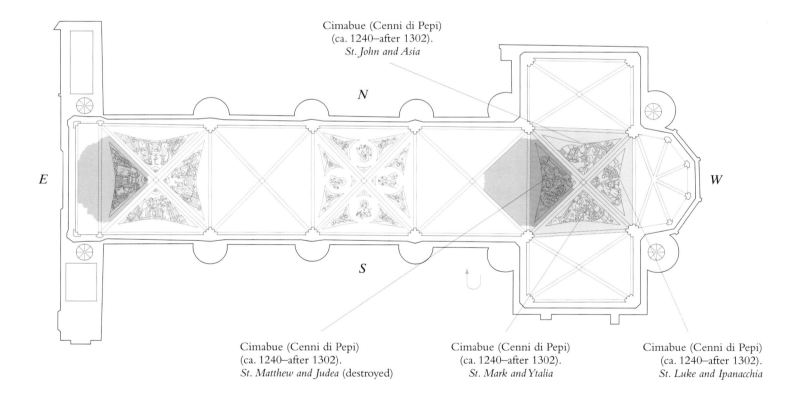

Cimabue (Cenni di Pepi)
(ca. 1240–after 1302).
St. John and Asia

N

E

W

S

Cimabue (Cenni di Pepi)
(ca. 1240–after 1302).
St. Matthew and Judea (destroyed)

Cimabue (Cenni di Pepi)
(ca. 1240–after 1302).
St. Mark and Ytalia

Cimabue (Cenni di Pepi)
(ca. 1240–after 1302).
St. Luke and Ipanacchia

Cimabue (Cenni di Pepi)
(ca. 1240–after 1302).
St. John and Asia

Cimabue
(Cenni di Pepi)
(ca. 1240–
after 1302).
*St. Matthew
and Judea*
(destroyed)

Cimabue
(Cenni di Pepi)
(ca. 1240–
after 1302).
*St. Luke and
Ipanacchia*

Cimabue (Cenni di Pepi)
(ca. 1240–after 1302).
St. Mark and Ytalia

41

42

43

Cimabue (Cenni di Pepi)
(ca. 1240–after 1302)
40 The vault of the Evangelists

Vault of the Evangelists

Cimabue (Cenni di Pepi)
(ca. 1240–after 1302)
41–43 Details of the fresco decoration of the
keystones of the vaults; south, west, and north sides

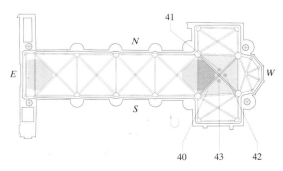

Vault of the Evangelists

Cimabue (Cenni di Pepi)
(ca. 1240–after 1302)
44 Vault section with *St. Matthew and Judea*
(destroyed)

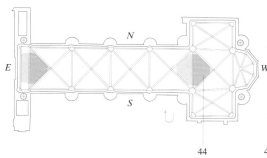

45

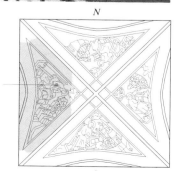

Vault of the Evangelists
Vault section with *St. Matthew and Judea* (destroyed)

Cimabue (Cenni di Pepi)
(ca. 1240–after 1302)
45 *St. Matthew*

S· MATHEUS·

JUDEA·

ÉVG ESTA

Vault of the Evangelists
Vault section with *St. Matthew and Judea*
(destroyed)

Cimabue (Cenni di Pepi)
(ca. 1240–after 1302)
46 *Judea*

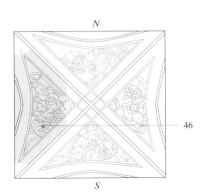

46

Vault of the Evangelists

Cimabue (Cenni di Pepi)
(ca. 1240–after 1302)
47 Vault section with *St. Mark and Ytalia*

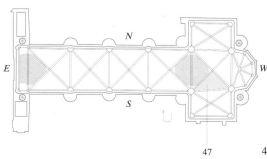

48

S. MARC·
EVGLSTA·
YTALIA

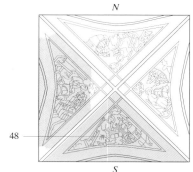

N

48

S

Vault of the Evangelists
Vault section with *St. Mark and Ytalia*

Cimabue (Cenni di Pepi)
(ca. 1240–after 1302)
48 *St. Mark*

49

Vault of the Evangelists
Vault section with *St. Mark and Ytalia*

Cimabue (Cenni di Pepi)
(ca. 1240–after 1302)
49 *Ytalia*

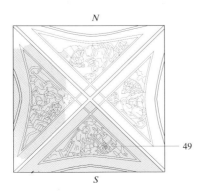

Vault of the Evangelists

Cimabue (Cenni di Pepi)
(ca. 1240–after 1302)
50 Vault section with *St. Luke and Ipanacchia*

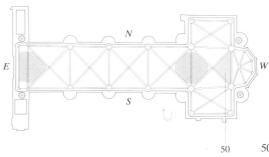

51

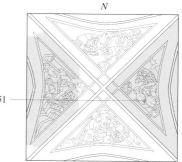

Vault of the Evangelists
Vault section with *St. Luke and Ipanacchia*

Cimabue (Cenni di Pepi)
(ca. 1240–after 1302)
51 *St. Luke*

EVGLSTA·

·IPNACC   HAIA·

Vault of the Evangelists
Vault section with *St. Luke and Ipanacchia*
Cimabue (Cenni di Pepi)
(ca. 1240–after 1302)
52 *Ipanacchia*

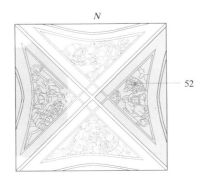

52

Vault of the Evangelists

Cimabue (Cenni di Pepi)
(ca. 1240–after 1302)
53 Vault section with *St. John and Asia*

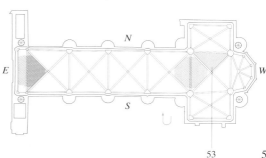

54

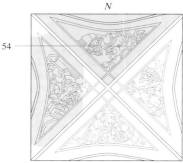

Vault of the Evangelists
Vault section with *St. John and Asia*

Cimabue (Cenni di Pepi)
(ca. 1240–after 1302)
54 *St. John*

EVGLSTA

ASIA

Vault of the Evangelists
Vault section with *St. John and Asia*
Cimabue (Cenni di Pepi)
(ca. 1240–after 1302)
55 *Asia*

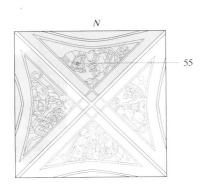

55

56

57

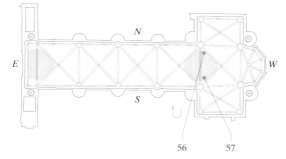

Vault of the Evangelists

Cimabue (Cenni di Pepi)
(ca. 1240–after 1302)
56, 57 Telamons

58

59

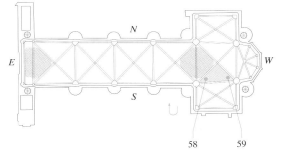

Vault of the Evangelists

Cimabue (Cenni di Pepi)
(ca. 1240–after 1302)
58, 59 Telamons

60

61

Vault of the Evangelists

Cimabue (Cenni di Pepi)
(ca. 1240–after 1302)
60, 61 Telamons

62

63

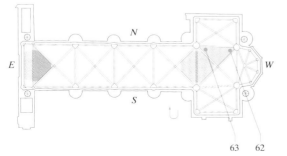

Vault of the Evangelists

Cimabue (Cenni di Pepi)
(ca. 1240–after 1302)
62, 63 Telamons

63   62

68

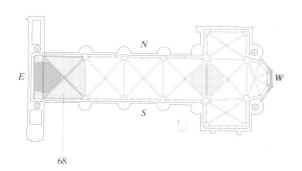

68 The vault of the Doctors of the Church, after the earthquake (Sestini photo)

68

69

69 The vault of the Evangelists, after the
earthquake (Sestini photo)

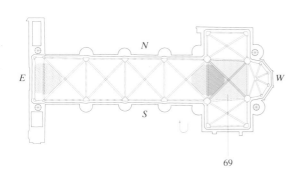

69